GOGIRL
You Have All It Takes

Loveth Omotola

Dedication

To Mum – my forever GoGirl

"Success is not male; success is not female. Success is a person; the person that dares"

Loveth Omotola

TABLE OF CONTENTS

Introduction

What would be, would be?

"The only person you are destined to be is the person you decide to be"

Ralph Waldo Emerson

And there it is; what would be, would be. This line of thought has put a lot of persons, both young and old in the backseat of their own lives. "What would be, would be" has left a lot of persons leaving their lives to chance, leaving their lives to the dictates of their environment, leaving their lives to the dictates of the circumstances around them, leaving their lives to the dictates of external conditions and watching their lives follow the winds of life in whatever direction it goes while they simply watch in self-pity and despair; feeling helpless or looking for help in the wrong places.

I once heard the story of two boys, twins; born into a family. These boys lived with their abusive father who was an alcoholic. When they grew up, one of the boys became an alcoholic. When asked why, he simply said "I watched my father". The other boy grew up to never drink even once in his life and when asked why, he said "I watched my father ". Two boys; same father, same family, same circumstance, different views, different choices, different actions, different results and different personalities.

So, what led to their emerging differences? The answer is simple; they saw and responded to their situation differently. One became a victim of his upbringing, while the other became a victor because he chose not to let his upbringing have a negative effect on his life, so as not to end up just like his father. He knew the direction he wouldn't want to go in life and that helped him find his own path and take charge of his own life. This one did not leave his life to chance.

Have you ever thought of this? You wake up in the morning, you do certain things to keep your body clean. Things like brushing your teeth, having your bath and wearing clean clothes. Why do you do all of these everyday? Simple! Because they are the necessary things you have to do in order to look good and smell nice each day. The moment you are no longer a child, you should know that these are the things you should do for yourself and by yourself without anyone having to remind you of them.

Just imagine you decide not to brush your teeth and have your bath for like a week and then you say ''what would be, would be''; You would have become a total mess of yourself. No one would consider you appealing, and no one would want to stay close to you. Keeping clean will not be; it is your responsibility to keep yourself clean and tidy.

You need to know this, what would be, would not be until you make it be or better still, what would be, would not be unless you allow it be. See it this way, say for instance, you are the driver of a car and have decided to go from Point A to B. You then begin your journey bearing in mind that your destination is Point B. Even if the car breaks down on the road, you will look for ways to repair the car and fix it in order to ensure that it's in perfect shape for the journey ahead.

Will you now say because the car got bad on the road, you will no longer carry on with getting to your destination? No you will not! Even if the route you are taking has a blockade ahead of it, you will remove the obstacle or better still, you find another route that will take you to your destination. All of this will be because you have made up your mind to get to your destination no matter what happens.

That's how to make things be in life, regardless of opposing factors. Whatever would be, you will have to make it happen. It's your choice to make. Whatever you will be, it's all up to you. Whatever might happen in your journey, it's up to you to choose to see the brighter side and decide to come out of it a better person with your dignity, strength, beauty and wholeness intact. It's up to you to not let your shoulders down and give in to defeat and let yourself be the convener of a pity party. It's all up to you.

How True This Is!

It is all up to you to make the beautiful life that you want. You should not leave your life to chance. You should not let the environment you find yourself confine and determine how successful you are going to be in life. You should not let your family background determine what will be of your life in the next ten years. The only thing that you should allow determine your life and future is you, the real you, who you are inside.

This is why you must invest in you. This is why you must feed this inner you with the right thoughts and thinking patterns; get trained in relevant life skills and get adequate knowledge that is required for this beautiful journey ahead, because everything originates first from the inside of you.

Talking about family background; that you were born to wealthy and influential parents is no guarantee that you will lead an impactful and successful life. If you do not make up your mind to use what you have to grow positively and become more than what you were born into, you will have to watch those things that were supposed to be to your advantage become your limitations.

Likewise, having a "less privileged" family background comes with its own demands. You don't have to get drowned in self-pity and the feeling of helplessness. You can write a new story. It's all up to you. Have you not heard of individuals who are now great men and women of influence and affluence that had to build from the very scratch? The choice was theirs to make.

Your choice is always yours to make. You have to understand that you are a unique person. There is no one in the whole world like you. Nobody can do the things you do like you do them. That makes you so special. You didn't happen by chance. There is a reason you came into this world. Once you discover it, you will live it and you will positively influence your world with it.

Just so you know, all that you need to live out your purpose has already been deposited inside of you. All you need to do now is uncover it, unleash it; unleash every raw talent, gift and potential that may be lying dormant, harness it, refine it until it becomes a beauty to behold; until it becomes a treasure to be sought after. That is the ultimate goal. Do you see why this inner you is priceless and should not be tampered with? Who you are inside is key.

You are the only person that can define you. Others who think they know you might try to define you but that is only to an extent. Nobody knows you like you do. The question of "Who am I?" is very personal to you. You need to know who you really are. When you know who you are, it will be easier to see where you and your special gift lies. It will be easier to see how you are different from every other person. You are the only person that can answer the question of who you are. Once you can answer it, it will give perspective to a whole lot of things. It will guide your choices, it will determine the kind of friends you make, it will set your standards and also set the course for your life.

That you are reading this book is a pointer that your journey into this beautiful life of self-discovery, self-actualization and self-mastery has started. There is a whole lot you will get to discover. So, come along, join me on this ride, let's explore this beautiful world together.

CHAPTER 1

INTEREST, PASSION AND COMMITMENT

"One person with passion is better than forty people merely interested"

E. M Forster

As a young girl, I was so inquisitive about the medical profession. I loved doctors because I saw them wear white, they looked clean and tidy, calm and calculated even in the face of pressure (as seen in the movies). At age six, when asked what my dream job would be, I said I wanted to be a medical doctor. But as I grew older and discovered more about the activities of doctors and what they go through in becoming a medical practitioner; including their training, I soon realized that there was more to this profession than just wearing white clothes, looking clean and appearing simple.

There was definitely more to it. Those things involved were the basics of the profession. Funny enough, those things that were considered basics, were the things I couldn't stand for a minute. I couldn't stand the smell in hospitals; I was disgusted at the sight of blood and I even detest the smell of drugs till date.

Now, knowing that these things can't be separated from doctors irrespective of their area of specialization, and that only those willing and ready to give it what it takes will become medical doctors eventually. Today, I simply admire doctors from afar. I sincerely respect and salute their courage, for in as much as I was interested in the medical profession, my interest wasn't strong enough to push me through the processes of becoming a medical doctor.

That was several years ago. Now, looking back, I get to ask myself certain questions as to what were the things that influenced the choice of that dream job as a child? I had mentioned earlier that it was because of how I saw the doctors dress, what they looked like and how they seemingly always look calm and calculated. This was all I could attach to the medical profession as a child.

So, what exactly was the motive behind my choice? My interest in the medical field was purely based on what I would look like and not because I wanted to help sick people get well or to ensure that more people got proper medical attention to minimize loss of lives. All my reasons for choosing the dream job were all superficial and that was because I was a child.

Being a child here does not only refer to being a toddler, it also points out to the lack of in-depth knowledge and the inability to make sound judgement and arrive at meaningful conclusions. This also can be likened to the possibility of people making certain decisions without accurate knowledge and therefore, the surety of concretized choices and actions cannot be achieved.

Childhood is a developmental stage of human growth. At this stage, a lot is yet to be fully formed as one is learning the basics through observation, experimentation and communication with the environment that one is. With the right supervision from an adult (one who is stable and mature in mind) mixed with accurate guidance and correction, the child is able to gain more knowledge and skills towards becoming more independent in thought and judgement. Thus, becoming more enhanced and able to make informed choices. When you are no longer a child, it is expected that you do away with childish things and become more conscious and intentional about the things that influence your interest for anything; that is, the real motives behind whatever it is that you have chosen to be or decided to do.

Being interested in something shouldn't just be about what you would look like being involved in it, it should be more of what you would make out of it. How you would use it to contribute your quota to the ever-increasing needs of mankind. As much as you should derive a sense of joy and fulfilment in it, it should be aimed at bringing more ease and joy to the people in your world.

What Then Is Interest?

Interest is that feeling which causes a special attention towards something. Interest is that which causes you to want to know and learn more about something; be it an activity, idea, profession or a cause. You cannot be said to be interested in something and not be informed of its modalities. Interest is that which will put you out there to test what you are good at, what you are not so good with and what you are willing to do. It is possible to be interested in a number of things. Once you put yourself into them, in no time, you should be able to decipher which will be for the now, which will stay with you for a long while and which one you are better off without. We all are wired differently; what strikes a chord in one person may most likely not to be what strikes a chord in another person. What will be a major interest for one person may not be a major interest for the other person. This is because of our uniqueness as individuals. When something becomes of a major interest to an individual, the intensity of interest in that thing can be said to have increased and that can be an indication that passion has come into play.

Passion

Passion describes a very strong liking or desire for something; a super admiration for an idea, cause, profession or an activity. It is always accompanied with this special kind of feeling of excitement that can be gotten from just the thought of something. Passion for something often reflects that there is that feature about you that resonates so well with that which you have such strong liking for. It's never a struggle and sometimes it's not something you consciously choose. It is usually something that you connect naturally with; something about you that just clicks so well that when you take it seriously and build on it, it becomes a part of you. In most cases, when someone takes something seriously and is always intense about it, that thing usually is a passion. It can be from the way or manner in which such activity, cause or profession is carried out. When you are passionate about something, it is possible that you almost feel like you can't do without it. When you are passionate about something, you will make time for it no matter how busy you are.

When you are passionate about something, you derive so much joy and fulfillment by just being involved in it. For example, if a person has a passion for volleyball, he or she will create time to play volleyball, watch the games, educate people about volleyball and eventually start training and building a team of volleyball players, even if he or she finds himself or herself in an environment with people who have little or no knowledge of the game. This is what passion is all about.

This individual may be involved with other things and may play other roles in a different industry of life but still have a way of blending in his passion with his everyday routine of life. This person lives and breathes his passion- volleyball and may even go to the extent of choosing a career related to volleyball as a sport. One can't have passion for so many things the way it is seen with interest. This is a key difference between interest and passion.

You see! Interest is not enough. It is one step close but not there yet. Amidst the many things that you are interested in, find something that you are passionate about and keep being interested in it. Does it sound a bit confusing? Let me shed more light on it. We can say that interest is simply liking something, while passion is an intense liking and admiration for something that pushes you to action.

So, when you know the things that you really like (the things that you are interested in), from among them, pick out one that you have intense admiration for; the one that gives you unexplainable excitement (the one that you are passionate about), then keep liking that particular one. In a nutshell, keep being interested in that which you are passionate about.

Remember, we said that interest is that which gets you to learn more and want to know more. Get to learn more of that which you are passionate about. Get to find out and know more about that which you are passionate about.

Passion is the springboard that launches you off to a more streamlined direction. "Follow your passion" is not just a cliché. It is an important decision you need to make. Let your passion lead you. If your passion for something doesn't get you to immerse yourself into it, then you might just forget about it and know that it is not for you. Passion comes with enthusiasm.

Passion propels you from the inside. It is nearly impossible to bottle up passion. It would be seen. It would be heard. People can literally feel it when they come around you. You can't even make a complete sentence without relating or making a reference to that which you are passionate about. Passion prepares your mind to put yourself into all that is required to live out that which you are intense about. Passion makes it possible for that which you are so excited about to become tangible to you.

So now, the million-dollar question is: What is your passion? You have got to discover this by yourself. What are you not just merely interested in? What are you willing to engage yourself with? What are you passionate about?

Passion means you love doing a certain activity so much that by practicing it, you lose yourself in that activity that you spend so much time on it without even realizing that you have skipped lunch. When you are at it, you are always full of energy and joy. Once you are passionate about something, you will want to know more, you will find out more, you will want to learn more, you will build and perfect your skills around it and you will watch it grow. Passion will give you a reason to open yourself to learning and to strive towards mastery. Passion will give you the needed courage to achieve the things you want most in life. It will give you the determination to conquer whatever it is that might sprout as an obstacle.

You will always find a way when there is passion. What you are passionate about has a way of making you look forward to tomorrow; making you look forward to living life. You now have something you live for. You now have something that is your gift to the world; something that is an extension of you to the rest of the world.

Now, It is no longer just about me, myself and I. It is more than you and your immediate environment. Just having a passion will make you set definite goals and make realistic plans to achieve them. This will keep your mind productively engaged, keep you looking for new ideas and how to make existing ones better. You have got to discover your passion. And as often as possible, practice the activities that surround your passion, invest in your passion; give it what it requires in time, learning and study. Watch it evolve.

Passion is that one thing that can keep you awake and happy while others are sleeping; that one thing that distinguishes you. Everybody around you know that when it comes to this particular thing, you are the first person that comes in mind. What are you passionate about? Find out that one thing.

This brings to mind one of my encounters with a secondary school girl. She just resumed classes in the senior secondary school and was majored in science subjects. During school club days, it was expected that science students go to JETS (Junior Engineers, Technicians and Scientists) club. She had no interest in the activities of the JETS club because for her, it was more like class work continued.

As time went on, she wasn't as active as expected in the club. She was more interested in the speech and debate club. Somehow, there was an opportunity to change clubs. Oh! She grabbed it with both hands. She was still a science student but then her school club was the speech and debate club. Her engagements with her new club gave her a lot of platforms to express herself more in speeches through relevant talk shows and debate competitions organized. This was an unveiling and sharpening of her persuasive skills and speech eloquence. This was the beginning of her journey as an excellent speaker and exceptional writer.

A lot of times, situations will not make it easy for you to pick on your interest. At times, what is considered the "norm" may not give you the opportunity to really express that which you are all about. However, interest and passion for something has a way of coming out; they have a way of showing up and becoming noticeable. It's just you staying true to yourself. It's just you being consistent with what you are about. Not today, it is this one and tomorrow, it is that one. Find out that one thing, stay true to it and stay consistent. Passion will take you on a journey; an uphill movement geared towards the sharpening and mastering of those attributes that come naturally with you.

Now that you are so interested in this thing, very passionate about it; how do you ensure that you do not deviate from it? What more do you need to ensure that come what may, you would stay on this. What more is necessary to stay on course? This is where commitment comes in, it is the sealing element.

Commitment

Commitment is that quality of being dedicated to a cause, profession or an activity. It is that state of being obligated or impelled towards something; a dedication towards becoming or achieving something irrespective of what may come. At this point, you are set on that which you have purposed to achieve, and you stick to it by all means and against all odds. Interest and passion collectively, must have revealed that which you like to do, that which you do not want to get involved with and that which you are willing to give your very best to. However, it takes commitment to take you through the journey of becoming.

Committing yourself to learning, committing yourself to the required training and committing yourself to all that it takes. Commitment streamlines your focus and directs your energy to the right channels so as to ensure you yield maximally in your chosen endeavour. Hear the stories of great men and women who have significantly achieved milestones in their lives, if there was anything that was their fire, it was their commitment to their passion that made them never to divert or cower in the face of glaring opposing elements. Commitment begins with a thoughtfully made choice and is sustained by dedication and perseverance. You are dedicated to your passion intellectually by giving it all that is required in learning, in training, in practice and in mastery. You are committed to your passion emotionally by ensuring that you build the necessary courage and willpower to pull through thick and thin. This is how you show commitment really. You don't exactly have to be talked into it and you don't need to be persuaded. You just know that this is it; this is what you need to do and this is the price you need to pay for this prize. This is the endeavour that you consider worthy.

That you are passionate about a thing does not mean that it would not come with its own share of challenges. Tests and trials will surface to put you off track. Your determination towards your passion and your commitment towards it both intellectually and emotionally should help get you back on track. Commitment is very active. Commitment is realized in thoughts and actions. You will become inseparable with the cause or endeavour that you have committed yourself to. Commitment is a must, if your passion will produce for you desired outcomes.

Let's put it this way. Interest is the teaser- the one that lets you play around and experiment with the things you like, passion is the stabilizer which brings more focus to what you are about while commitment is the deal maker; this is the one that signs and stamps the cheque that you can now take to the bank. Commitment gets you paid. Commitment gives to you the desired results. You've got to complete the full package as they come in phases. You've got to follow your passion and let your passion lead you. You've got to commit to your passion. You've got to live out your passion!

All of these boils down to; Who are you? What are you about? What do you love to do? What are you good at? What are you interested in? What are you passionate about? What are you committed to? Just know this, it is at the interplay of your power, your uniqueness, your interest, your passion and your commitment that your purpose lies; either it is discovered, or it is created.

Here is the trick, create your purpose around your passion or discover your purpose around your passion.

Passion and purpose is like a jigsaw puzzle, you know what you want and every other thing will fall into place.

It all depends on you.

CHAPTER 2

MANAGING YOUR MIND

''If you think you can do a thing or think you can't do a thing, you are right''

Henry Ford

The human mind is a very powerful instrument. The use of it can make or mar, can build or destroy and can give life or cause death; depending on how it is used. The quality and character of your mind is what describes the inner you; the real you. This real you is a major determinant for the successes you are going to experience in this life. The inner you which is the real you is where your emotions stream from; where your will power originates from, where your intelligence comes from, where your confidence roots from, where your reasoning sits, where your courage resides and where your thoughts dwells.

All of these features aforementioned form the very core of every man; this makes up the real man and this is the real deal. When people relate with you, as much as they relate with your physical body, their description of you on the long run is always of their encounter with the real you; your reasoning and your real character which makes up a higher percentage when they are to describe you.

The Container; The Content

Let us look at this illustration. Say for instance, you got five bottles of water and you empty each one of them. You poured milk into the first bottle; you poured liquid soap into the second bottle; you poured kerosene into the third bottle; you poured petrol into the fourth bottle and lastly, you poured cooking oil into the fifth bottle. Now, place all of these bottles on the same table marking each one with what they contain. When you are asked to bring milk from the table, it is the bottle of milk that you will get. Right? Absolutely Yes! If you are asked to bring liquid soap from the table, you will most likely get the bottle of liquid soap. They are all bottles, but they now contain different things; what the bottles contain is what describes the bottle.

You need to understand this. There is the container and there is the content; it is the content that describes the container and not the other way round. Have you ever had this funny encounter where you pick up a container labelled milk from the shelf; the write up on the container says it is milk that is inside and then you open it, only to find sugar inside. Is that a container of milk or a sugar container? Of course, it is a sugar container. It doesn't matter what is written on the container, it is what is inside it that tells us exactly what it is. It is possible that it was milk that was originally in that container but when the milk finished, somebody in the house used the container to store sugar. It is also possible that milk is written on the container and then you also find milk inside the container too.

However, you will now come to agree with me that it is the content that eventually describes the container. Likewise, it is what is inside a man that describes the man. The man inside a man is the real man. The inner you is the real you.

Having A Mind Set

Having established that the quality and character of your mind describes the real you, it is important to note that this real you is your responsibility; that it is up to you to build the character and the quality of your mind. The mind can be set, and your mindset is your responsibility. You decide what you want to build and the quality you will get. This is where the differences in the results that people have stem from.

Ever wondered why some people tend to lead more successful lives than others. This is mostly because of the programming of their mind; the way their minds have been set, the information that they have come to accept and live by, the habits they have formed over time and what they have believed as possible or impossible. It all starts in the mind. The mind is not a tangible part of the human body that can be seen and touched like the eyes, kidneys and the rest of them. If you get a doctor to dissect a human body, there is no part of the body, be it external or internal that can be displayed as the mind.

This is because the mind is an integral part of the inner man. Can the inner man be seen? No, the inner man can't be seen. We can only relate with the inner man through the workings of the mind. It is through the mind that we are able to comprehend information, to form opinions, to have intentions through our interactions and then process information in such a way as to arrive at conclusions.

This means that every human has a mind of their own; everyone can use their minds to give meaning to things, images, languages, information and expressions as the case may be. How each and every one of us give interpretation to things, would be to the extent of the quality training, learning and exposure that our minds have received with regards to the subject matter. Say for instance, a mind that has not been trained to understand Chinese Language will hear sounds and words but cannot attach any meaning to them. It will all sound strange, funny and foreign since this particular mind has not been exposed to hearing and learning Chinese Language.

Even in some of our schools that now teach French as a language, do you remember the first day your French teacher came to class and started speaking French language to the whole class. Some of you even laughed at all that the teacher said. But, over time, with continuous exposure and learning, your mind got familiar with the vocabulary of the language and no longer consider it funny. This is because your mind has been equipped to an extent to recognize and give meaning to letters and words of the French Language.

In fact, whatever we know is as a result of what our minds has been taught or the information that we have come to accept. So, it is the mind that interprets and gives meaning to what is heard and seen. Through training and the right learning, accompanied with relevant exposure, the mind can be equipped to interpret and give meaning to things, images, languages, information and expressions accordingly.

Various people have different mindset which can be as a result of their different exposure, their different training, their different learning and the difference in the things that they have come to accept. These differences streams from their different mindset. The word "mindset" used here should ring a bell, as it connotes that the mind can be set; replacing what was with what should be; adjusted accordingly to give the desired quality of thoughts because the mind functions with thoughts.

Your Thoughts

Thoughts go through your mind. The kind of thoughts that go through your mind and what you do with those thoughts is very important. The kind of thoughts that you dwell on makes a whole difference in your life as you are the expression of your thoughts.

A lot of times, thoughts come in form of imaginations resulting from information that brings us to creating pictures in our minds and dwelling on them. The power of our thoughts should never be underestimated especially when given vent. One cannot be separated from the contents of his or her thoughts. You are your thoughts and your thoughts are you. As a man thinks, so he is. As a woman thinks, so she is. As a boy thinks, so he is. As a girl thinks, so she is. Every single individual is a product of their own thoughts. Until you can change your thoughts and thinking patterns, you cannot change the direction of your life.

You have to know this; your life is always in the direction of your thoughts. Someone might ask, where do these thoughts even come from? They come from the information and communication that you have been exposed to. It might be in the books that you read, the things you often listen to, the movies that you see and the conversations you have had. This is why you must be very selective of the materials that you feed your mind with. In whatever form that they come, be sure that they are of good quality and character.

A thought is considered of good quality when its contents build you rightly and make you a better person afterwards. A thought is considered not to be of good quality when it cripples the productivity of your mind and impairs your ability to see positivity. These kinds of thoughts are dangerous and destructive to your life.

Quality information and communication breeds quality thoughts. However, if not so good thoughts come to you, it is your sole responsibility to discard it immediately. You owe it to yourself to mount guard over the thoughts that come into your mind. Dwell on only quality thoughts and discard every thought that is not of quality character.

Just like that farmer who plants edible vegetables in his farm and expects a bounty harvest. When unwanted weeds grow on his farmland, he uproots them; he rids off his farm regularly of any weed that he doesn't want. Similarly, on a regular basis, clear your mind.

Consciously, remove thoughts that are not needful and replace them with the thoughts that are valuable. Do away with thoughts that do not build you, thoughts of fear, thoughts of failure and thoughts of penury. Do away with them. Dwell on thoughts of confidence, thoughts of success and thoughts of abundance. The quality of life you would live here on Earth is largely dependent on the quality of the contents of your thoughts.

How To Measure Good Thoughts

There is a standard to which the character and quality of thoughts can be measured. These are the criteria in which the thoughts that meet them can be ascertained to be of good quality and standard. So, when information comes to you and then you begin to build thoughts around them, you should ask yourself these questions. These are questions that if your thoughts answer "YES" to, you will be so sure that your thoughts are of good quality and standard, for you to now dwell on them. With respect to the information that has come to you, the questions are:

Is it Honest? Oh! If it is honest, Is it Just? Oh! If it is just, Is it Pure? Oh! If it is pure, Is it Lovely? Oh! If it is lovely, Is it of Good Report? Oh! If it is of good report, Is there any Virtue? Oh! If there is any virtue, Is there any Praise?

So, here is your checklist. The thoughts that answer "YES" to all of these questions are the thoughts you should let occupy your mind and control the way you think. These are the thoughts that you should process. This is how you separate and select the thoughts that come to you.

This should be your checklist for quality assurance and control of your thoughts.

Honest√ Just√ Pure√ Lovely√ Good Report√ Virtuous√ Praiseworthy√

Any thought that you should dwell on should have a pass mark of each of these criterions. At this point, you are certain of its quality assurance.

Be more conscious of positivity. Be more aware of the good around you. Be more aware of the good that can be possible around you. See the good in everyone. See the good in everything. When you make up your mind to see only the good, you will see only good. Trust me, positivity brings good tidings.

Even when it looks like all is not well, always have the mind that choose to focus on only the good or the mind that choose to make the bad to become good. Use your mind right for the right things you want to happen for you and your environment. It is your life that we are talking about here. This is the way to have a beautiful life. You must first cultivate an excellent mind.

If you carry all the negativities of this world and bombard your mind with them, what good will it do you? Unless you are thinking productively on how to switch the "negatives" to "positives", which is what creative thinking is all about.

An excellent mind is possible; a mind that is devoid of negative thoughts and negativity. A mind full of love, joy, hope, kindness, happiness and beauty is achievable. This is the goal. If you get it right from your mind, you got all things right.

Meditation is Key

Now that you are able to select your thoughts, it is important that you know the role of meditation. Meditation refers to a conscious deep reflection of your thoughts; it is the grooming of your thoughts in such a manner that it becomes your every second reality and it becomes so real to you. You ruminate around your thoughts, ideas, goals, plans, dreams and visions until all that you see is possibilities and a thousand ways it can be achieved.

Meditation is a continuous exercise. It is actually a lifestyle. It demands that you separate yourself be it physically, mentally or both, from everyone and everything. You take yourself to that realm where nobody else but you and only you get your undivided attention. This is your creation time. Also, you should be with writing materials at that point because a lot of good thoughts will come to your mind and you will need to write them down, word for word so you don't miss out on any detail. For some of us, meditation is not something that can occur in a rowdy place; that would mean too many distractions as it calls for serenity. This is our quiet times; times that we separate ourselves from everyone and everything to be alone, quiet the heart and focus the mind so we can capture our thoughts.

Over the years, this has helped me to relax my mind and then because my mind is more relaxed, I can think more clearly and creatively. This is where I also dwell and build on beautiful thoughts. Thoughts that would give more meaning to my life and the life of others. Thoughts that would make my world a better place. For me, it has to be a quiet place, devoid of any form of noise or distraction. For some others, they may require some kind of activity in the background. Whichever way, you may just need to find out what works best for you and stick with it. Just know it is alone time.

And at such a time, do not rush your thoughts, give it time to build up, give it time to be clearer, give it time to build substance, give it time to be shaped. Keep fine tuning them. The most assured way to do this is to put your thoughts into writing. No matter how silly it may sound at first, write it down. By the time you are done with fine tuning, you will be amazed of what you have made out of the assumed silly thought.

In the place of meditation, you get yourself to the point where you begin to visualize; you see and create pictures in your mind of all that you want to change, of all you want to achieve and all that you want to become. You give them form and colour in the pictures that you create. It is in the place of meditation that visualization begins. For instance, if you want to be a successful professional athlete, all you have to do is to see yourself taking those perfect strides as you run, see your feet barely touching the ground on the track.

As you practice your techniques, see yourself being the best of you every day. Visualize yourself lifting that trophy as the champion that you are. This way, you will be stimulating your mind towards achieving your desired goals. Until you see it, it won't become real to you and until it becomes real to you, you can't take a hold of it. As far as you can see and take a hold of, that's what you will have. This takes place during meditation.

Personally, quiet times are best in the early hours of the day when I am just waking up from sleep. This is most likely the best alone time I might have, as most people around will probably still be asleep. It is also a great start for the day as it always helps me set the tone for the rest of my day. When my mind is ready for the day, then I know that I am ready to have a wonderful day. Then, in between my work schedule for the day, when the opportunity to be alone shows up, I don't hesitate.

You can also consciously decide to take a few minutes from your day to meditate on quality thoughts as it relates to your life, family, work, school and the list goes on and on. Meditation keeps you in sync with your innermost cogitations. Take full advantage of it.

Affirmations

These are positive assertions and declarations of that which you want and of who you are. Those things which you have seen in your times of meditation. This is the time to declare them and to affirm them. Through meditation, you are able to saturate your mind with the right thoughts. Through visualization, you are able to see and create your realities and through affirmations, you declare these realities. This is the point where you begin to talk it, first to yourself and to anyone who gets to ask. It's part of your alone time activities. You talk these realities into being. Remember that this is a lifestyle. It is not a trial and error kind of thing. These things work. I know because this is the life that I have lived for over a decade now and my only regret is that I wish I knew about this kind of life earlier on in my life. But then, I am a super grateful for the time that I came to the knowledge of this reality.

I have watched the lives of great men and women of substance; this is how they live and rule their world. It is a conscious and intentional lifestyle. See, success is never a mystery. It is the application of already tested and proven principles. When you see someone being successful at something and you get to find out how they did it. If you apply the same principles, it is most likely that you get similar results.

Did you notice that I said that if you apply the same principles not if you do the same things they did. This is because doing the same things they did may not work for you, you might not exactly get it that way but then if you find out the principles that are behind their action and apply accordingly as it pertains to you, it is most sure that you will get your desired results in your own unique way.

There's a whole lot that depends on you. You can't let you down.

What you say concerning you truly matters. In fact, what you say about you matters more than what anybody says about you. So, you got to talk to yourself more. Do not be reluctant to declare what you are and who you are. Even if it is not what you are experiencing at the moment, use your mouth to say it into being. Show yourself some love and give yourself some hope. You may not get anybody to speak some real good thing to your life.

Even if you have someone declaring some goodies about you, it is often the ones that you declare to yourself that will hold more because it will be more regular as you are always with you. Whatever your affirmation is about, ensure to always declare it in the present tense and not in future tense because it is your present minute reality.

If your affirmation is about your health, do not say "I will be healthy" instead say "I am healthy". If your affirmation is about your grades in school, don't say "I will be an A+ student" instead say "I am an A+ student".

I call this the "Mirror exercise". I get a full-length mirror or a face mirror (depending on which is available) and talk to the person that I see in the mirror. For me, while looking into the mirror, I say things like:

- I am beautiful
- I am happy
- I am super intelligent
- I am confident and bold
- I am full of Love
- I can get what I want
- I am healthy and wealthy
- I am smart and vibrant
- I am full of life
- I am the best of me
- I influence this world positively......

And it can go on and on.

You can create your own affirmations as it is peculiar to you; write them down and read them to yourself until you master them so much that you wouldn't need to recite them from a piece of paper. They become a part of you. Even if you are to wake up in the middle of the night, you can say them without reading from any book. You can also decide to represent your affirmations in pictures, sketches and images; you can place them in your room or somewhere your eyes would constantly see them staring at you. This will inspire your everyday endeavour and It will serve as a beautiful reminder of all that you must achieve and who you are becoming.

My dear friends, the beautiful life is all yours. All you have to do is think it, see it, talk it, walk in it and live it.

It is all up to you.

CHAPTER 3

YOUR DRIVE

I figured if a girl wants to be a legend, she should go ahead and be one

Martha Jane Canary

Imagine a man who just got a new car. Everything in the car is in good shape, good working condition and the car is fuel. Then, the man gets into the car, sits on the driver's seat and do nothing. Few minutes later, you hear the man grumbling and complaining that the car isn't moving.

What would you think of this man? I would think that the man has definitely missed something out. Because, when one gets on the driver's seat of a sound car, you do not expect the car to move by itself. So, what do you do? You turn on the ignition either by inserting the car keys or by pressing a button. This is how you give power to the car in order for it to get into motion; in order for it to move.

In the same vein, your drive is the power required to put all that you have and all that you are together so that you can get moving to your desired destination or towards achieving that which you have purposed to do. This is the push from within that is necessary; the motivation that is needed.

Ignite From Within

Using the illustration of the car, bear in mind that all the car needed to move was already inside the car. There was not any need for it to depend on external features. This is to say that what drives you should first come from within. Your motivation should primarily originate from inside of you and not from anything or anyone external. Someone or something might influence it, but it has to gain roots on the inside of you. It is called, "Self-Motivation".

Self-motivation is lighting your own fire, knowing what makes you thick and continually engaging in practices that elevate and make you dependent on yourself to make things happen.

Over time, self-motivation has proven to be the best and most reliable form of motivation anyone can have. As you can always at anytime and anywhere depend on you. Self-motivation works with the underlying principle that all that is within you is capable of producing what you need around you. Self-motivation sees ability in you at whatever level that you are now.

Know this, champions are first champions from within. Greatness often begins from within. If you are going to shine, it has to begin from within you; from the inside of you. Light up from within. Make sure you light your own fire and let it burn from inside where nothing and no one except you can determine how long it will burn and the intensity of which it will burn. Never forget that you spend more time with you; you are always with you.

Becoming Self Motivated

When everyone and everything else is gone, you will always have you. So, it is imperative that you make you a reason to keep going. Becoming a self-motivated individual is a continuous process that can keep building up when one engages in the right exercise. Here, these exercises have been summarized in three steps:

1.   ***Love yourself:*** You have to learn to love yourself. You have to see yourself as smart, capable, talented and wise. In you are so much positive traits. You have to accept yourself as these. Until you see them for yourself, you may never realize how special, unique and powerful you are. Always take a realistic look at yourself and intentionally focus on the positive traits that you possess. Those glaring positive traits that you have are what works for you. So, work with them. Work with what works for you; always wake up each new day with your greatest assets sharpened and ready to conquer new grounds. This will build your confidence. Remember, you are the only one like you.

2.   ***Know that you are enough:*** Always bear in mind that who you are inside is all that you need to get all that you want. You are enough. Be better everyday; make a conscious effort to learn something new everyday. Add to your knowledge daily. Strive to be better than you were yesterday. There is always room for improvement. The you that is enough, calls for regular development. Whatever you are going to be, you are already becoming. What you do so often, build up and form the character of your

personality. So, keep getting better and know that you are enough.

3.   ***Never compare:*** When people compare themselves with others, it often points out that they have an unhealthy self-esteem. If you really know who you are; your worth and your value, you will never have to compare your results and achievements with somebody else's. We are all very unique and special in our different ways. Hence, comparison is an absolute waste of time and energy. Imagine a razor blade comparing itself with a cutlass. Funny, right? There is an African adage that says, "the razor blade is so sharp but it can't cut a tree; the cutlass is so strong but can't cut your hair". See! They have their places. Find your lane, stay in your lane and proceed to win. Know this for real, you are not in any competition with anybody. The only person that you should want to be better than is the person you were yesterday. Be the best version of you.

When you keep doing these things, over time, you will come to realize that your self-motivation level keeps increasing and keep getting stronger. And then your strongest motivation is always within.

Stay Aglow

It is one thing to be lighted up and it is another thing to stay aflame; to keep the fire burning. Do you know that happy people are glowing people? Yes, they are! Individuals who often carry a joyful atmosphere around tend to cover more grounds with ease and they achieve more within a short period.

Firstly, to stay aglow, you must always choose to be a happy person. Underline the word "chose". It is a deliberate choice actually because, things might happen or even people might happen too and then you may feel unhappy. There is this erroneous belief that happiness is somewhere out there or it's in something or its in someone else. A lot of people associate happiness with reaching a set goal or with acquisition of something. When you link your happiness to something you are yet to acquire, you are practically denying your power to create happiness for yourself.

When you set goals and achieve them, it should get you excited and more confident to achieve greater feats. The other way round, if things don't go as planned or expected, go back to your drawing board, remain happy and optimistic with your eyes set on the goal. Always remember that happiness is a place to come from and not a place we try to go. Where you are is where happiness is. Come from happiness to whatever you do; come from happiness to whatever you want to achieve; come from happiness to whoever you want to become. Let happiness express itself from the start and make your journey exciting all the way, not just at the end.

Secondly, to stay aglow, practice living in the moment. Don't live in the past or worry about the future - stay focused on today. Don't be that "I shouldn't have", "why did I", "I could have", "what if it doesn't work" kind of person. Don't have regrets and don't have doubts. Pay attention to today, on now. What should I do now? How can this getter better now?

Learn to live in the here and now. Of course, there is the place for creative thinking, planning and goal setting. These are important. Nevertheless, when you are through with all of that, pay attention and focus on the present hour. Break your goals into bits; from yearly, to monthly, to weekly, to daily, to hourly and to every minute. Make the most of the present moment, this moment right now is your purest opportunity. What are you going to do with it? Take it one minute at a time, one hour at a time, one day at a time and make it count.

Confronting Fear

Ever heard that at the other side of fear lies all we want to achieve. This insinuates that fear is most likely the only thing that keeps anyone from achieving any given feat. Fear often arise from negative or wrong information that one has been exposed to. People are most of the times afraid of what they don't even know. When people lose control over a situation or over something, panic sets in and then fear takes over. When they can't understand the happenings around them, panic sets in and fear takes over.

Over time, people have devised several methods of handling fear. Some avoid it by running away from it while it still keeps chasing them. It keeps hunting them, they have become preys of fear. Some others shut their eyes to it and pretend it doesn't exist. Thus, ending up in their darkest comfort zones. There is never any real way to run away from fear; as the more you run, the more pervasive it gets.

People develop fear for various things; fear of rejection (as being accepted validates them), fear of heights (they are afraid of falling), fear of insects (how do I even explain this?), fear of failure (as they are not certain they will rise from the setback) and countless others that may not be mentioned here. But at the top of all of these is the "fear of fear".

Let me explain this one, most times, it is not what is feared that causes havoc, it is always the degree at which fear has enveloped such individual, that at the slightest exposure to that which causes fear for them, that individual becomes a victim.

Do you know that you can live above fear? To fear is one thing, but to allow fear play hide-and-seek with you, that is a big issue.

I once heard a speaker tell his story. As a little boy, he was so afraid of crossing busy roads. It was so bad that each time he wants to cross a busy road, he would see himself being knocked down by a moving vehicle and dying at the spot. This image of being dead before he gets to the other side of the road kept hunting him until one day, he got to a crossroad, the awful scene played out in his mind again but this time around he changed it, since he is in charge of his mind. In this new scene, he tried crossing the road, was hit by a vehicle but then he somersaulted three times in the air, landed on his feet and finished crossing the road. He is alive! He did not die! That was the last time that fear showed up. So, what did the speaker do differently? He overcame the fear, first in his mind. That's how to confront fear. It's like saying "bring it on", I am coming out of this victorious. It's like saying "it doesn't matter the fiery darts you throw at me, none of it will hit me". That's the courageous mind. Courage disarms fear. You need to be courageous.

The great African Statesman, Nelson Mandela once said that:

"courage was not the absence of fear, but the triumph over it; the brave man is not one who does not feel afraid, but one who conquers that fear"

You need to overcome that which you fear. Let me ask you a question? What are you going to do if you are not afraid? What? Really? What? Go ahead and do them. Do not let fear stop you from learning new things. Do not let fear stop you from trying new things. Do what you need to do. Repeat these words after me: "fear has got nothing in me". Yes! Fear has got nothing in you.

You will do exploits. Always believe in yourself.

CHAPTER 4

YOUR CORE VALUES

"It is not hard to make decisions when you know what your values are"

Roy Disney

What are those things that are important to you? Why do you consider them important? Are there activities you engage in that make you feel that you were born just for them? What is so special about those activities? Do they leave you feeling fulfilled and satisfied? If your answer to the last question is YES, it can be said without an iota of doubt that what you are doing is settling the demands of one, if not all of your personal core values.

I must be quick to point out that the answer to the above questions would differ from person to person. What is considered important to Mr John is likely not to be so for Mr James. What Mr John derives fulfillment and satisfaction from might not be the same for Mr James. This stems from the fact that values are unique to individuals.

Whether we know it or not, each and every one of us have a set of values which to a large extent directs our perspective to everything in life as a whole. These are our core values.

What Are Core Values?

Core values are simply stable long-lasting beliefs about what is important to an individual; they are the base for which an individual can explore what is important to him or her and not what is important to other people. Core values are very personal. As a person, core values reveal what really matters to you; they reflect the fundamental choices of who you want to be. Your personal core values can make an amazing difference in how you live your life. So, it is important that you consciously identify what your core values are. In fact, the earlier you are aware and acquainted with what your core values are, it becomes easier for you to make the best choices in all aspects of your life.

There are numerous values to begin with. If you are not sure of what your values might be, here is a checklist of some core values that will give you some food for thought.

Please be reminded that there is just a few of these values that can be mentioned in this write up; if there is any value that is particular to you and is missing in this checklist, be free to add them to your list.

This is just to give you an idea of what values are. The topmost of these for you are your personal core values. How do you identify them? Keep reading, you are just about to find out.

Excellence **Brilliance**	**Creativity**	**Motivation**
Learning **Relationship**	**Simplicity**	**Success**
Integrity **Dedication**	**Being the best**	**Calmness**
Love **Empathy**	**Happiness**	**Making a difference**
Spirituality **Family**	**Leadership**	**Personal Development**
Charity **Resourcefulness**	**Boldness**	**Collaboration**
Service **Fairness**	**Professionalism**	**Innovation**
Health **Humility**	**Inspiration**	**Originality**

Ethics	Wisdom	Honesty
Diversity		
Adventure	Wealth	Expressiveness
Beauty		
Peace	Abundance	Fame
Friendship		
Quality	Appreciation	Wellbeing
Responsibility		
Passion	Optimism	Punctuality
Enthusiasm		
Balance	Selflessness	Pro activity
Vision		

Discovering Your Core Values

I have outlined six steps to guide you in identifying your personal core values, they include:

i. Get pen and paper, generate a list of your core values. You need to do some critical thinking here.

ii. From the core values that you have selected, put values that are alike in one group; you should have at least five groups after doing the grouping.

iii. From each group, select only one value that can serve as a representative for the rest in that same group.

iv. Be very selective here, you would end up with your top core values. If you had five groups, you should have five top core values now.

v. Then, take each top core value, summarize what it means to you personally and why it matters. Write your definition alongside each value.

vi. Prioritise these top values; know which comes before which.

And there you have it, your personal core values.

Your personal core values will guide your journey to living that life that is uniquely right and fulfilling for you. Also, be flexible enough to adjust as some of your values will probably change with time. As every phase of life comes with its own demands of you, make sure to make room for such changes. Now to the question, what are my personal core values? Following the above-mentioned steps, this is how I get to find out my own core values.

• Generating a list of my core values: Excellence, Optimism, Personal Development, Service, Humility, Honesty, Innovation, Originality, Wellbeing, Learning,

Charity, Beauty, Appreciation, Wealth, Success, Simplicity, Relationship, Happiness, Honour, Responsibility, Empathy, Inspiration, Love, Spirituality, Beauty, Balance.

• Put similar values in a group:

- Excellence, Originality, Innovation, Success, Simplicity.

- Personal Development, Learning, Responsibility, Inspiration, Optimism.

- Honesty, Appreciation, Honour.

- Wealth, Beauty, Wellbeing, Spirituality, Balance.

- Love, Humility, Service, Empathy, Charity, Relationship, Happiness.

• Being more selective of one that can represent others in the group, my top core values are: Excellence, Personal development, Honesty, Wealth and Love.

And now I summarize what each of these core values mean to me personally and why it matters.

Excellence is being more, not settling for average, standing out, being the best version of the real me, adding top notch value and it matters to me because I consider it the baseline of outstanding landmarks and successes.

Personal development is me being better, knowing better and doing better than my yesterday; it's me conquering new grounds, having a broader perspective to issues of life, taking up new roles and higher responsibilities; it matters to me because I know I can't be more than what I know and I can't give what I don't have.

Honesty is Power, as I will often say that I am most powerful when I am honest. There is dignity and honour in being honest. Honesty is being true first to myself and then staying true to my environment.

Wealth is the abundance of every good thing; beauty, sound health, spirituality and finding a balance in all of these that none should suffer at the expense of the other.

Love is that endearing ability that pushes me to leave an indelible positive impact on others. Love possess several other virtues like patience, kindness, service, humility and the rest. Love matters so much to me as it is my greatest motivation.

• Prioritizing my top core values: Love, Personal Development, Excellence, Wealth and Honesty.

And there it is, my topmost personal core values. Now, because I am ever conscious of them, it won't be so much difficult to make decisions. Whatever that does not satisfy and fulfil at least one of my top core values will not be attractive to me.

When you are clear about your core values, you are clear about what's important to you. Ensure you take this exercise of find your personal core values too, so you can be certain what should influence your choices and actions.

Actions and Consequences

Every day, we have choices to make and each choice is often followed up by actions, these actions do have corresponding results or consequences. For instance, if you chose not to sleep when you should, as a consequence, you will feel tired and worn out. If you chose not to eat when you should, as a consequence, you will feel hungry and maybe fatigued.

Likewise, if you chose not to study, especially if you are a student, as a consequence, you will not do well in your subjects or courses and eventually not pass your examinations in flying colours.

Making a choice is like picking up a stick; when you pick up one end of a stick, the other end always come with it. In other words, when you make a decision, a corresponding consequence usually follows. With this, it can be said that you are free to choose but are not free from the consequences of your choice. Many times, when the word "consequence" is used, it is usually tied to a negative outcome. It shouldn't be so. Consequences are simply follow-up results of a choice or an act. Good choices have consequences; bad choices have consequences too. So, choose rightly. This is why you must have personal core values; they aid your choices and decision making.

When making decisions that has got to do with any aspect of your life, it is important that you do not be majorly influenced by third parties; let those things that really matter to you guide your choices because in the long run, after all is said and done, nobody else but you will face the consequences of the choice that was made- whether wrong or right.

What you chose will choose you; the choices you make eventually makes you and not the people that influenced the choice for you. I often tell myself that I always want to look in the mirror and tell myself "girl, you did this to yourself, how can you fix it" when the consequence of a choice goes haywire or I tell myself "I am proud of you girl" when the consequence of a choice comes out beautiful. That's being responsible for your life and not looking for who to blame. Some consequences come immediately after a choice is made while some surface long after a choice or decision has been made and even forgotten. But eventually, there is always a consequence. So, it is important that you choose wisely.

Your Beliefs = Your Values = Your Core values = Your Choices = Your Actions = Consequences

Remember that your strong held beliefs build up to form your values, your core values guide your choices, your choices determine your actions and your actions have their consequences. That is the ripple impact. So, get it right from its foundation; your beliefs, the programming of your mind- your mindset. This is where it all begins.

CHAPTER 5

YOUR WALL

"If you don't set a baseline standard for what you will accept in life, you will find it's easy to slip into behaviours and attitude or a quality of life that is far below what you deserve"

Tony Robins

Walls are often structures that define or demarcate an area for the purpose of shelter, security and for setting boundaries. Walls separate areas for easy identification. When we bring this to human relations, walls are laid down principles, standards and rules set by each individual or a group as to what is acceptable to them. These self-set principles and standards tell so much about each and every one of us in the most unique ways.

Your walls are your standards; they are the self-set rules that guide the affairs of your life- your own laid down rules on how you treat yourself, how others should treat you, what you can tolerate and how you respond to your environment. It determines who you let in and what you let into the things that has got to do with you. It also streamlines what you accommodate. Your walls control the attitudes and behaviours that you will come to display and accept but most importantly, it is also a pointer to the quality of life that you will settle for. This is in the sense of the manner to which you conduct yourself.

Having Quality Standards

It is necessary to note that the most important standards you will have as an individual has a lot to deal with your own conduct- your own behaviour. How you treat your own self is mostly a reflection of what you think of yourself-a reflection of how much you value your person. When you consciously affect this area positively, all other aspects will be influenced likewise. This is first one of the ways you teach people how to treat you, how to deal with you and what to bring around you. This has got to do with how you act towards yourself; it is more of behavioural. Always know your expectations of you and always try to meet those expectations.

When you constantly set base rules for your own self and then you live up to them, you are training yourself to become a standard; a standard for you and a standard for the people you relate with; to come to respect especially when they are with you. There are basic standards for life and for success. Nonetheless, you have to clearly define what you want out of life. This is necessary in order to build the standards that are required for your peculiar journey of success.

To get started with being a person of good standard, there are three factors that you must take seriously.

1. ***Staying true to yourself***: Simply put, this means being real; being authentic. Being true means seeking honesty and integrity in all that has got to do with you. Staying true to yourself means staying consistent with your core values because your values are the foundation for building your standards and principles for life. Those things that are important to you, you have got to always act on them. When you are true to yourself, it will be very easy to be true to the people around you. When you are true to yourself, it will be easy to maintain and sustain a behavioural pattern. You are not pretending to be what you are not. You are always

you and then you are working towards a better you, one day at a time.

2. ***Be more aware of your values:*** The standards that you will live by are based on your values as an individual. When you become more conscious of your values; having them at your fingertips, it becomes more natural for you to slip into behaviours that align with them. Let's take my personal core values for example, they are love, personal development, excellence, wealth and honesty. Because I am more conscious of each one of them, I can't have a behaviour pattern that do not match with them. All my principles and standards in one way or the other had got to reflect my values. My standards revolve around self-confidence which can be tied to personal development, integrity which is related with honesty, courage as it connects with positivity and love which is my greatest motivation. It is impossible that my actions are not governed by these. This is what it means to know who you are and stay true to who you are.

3. ***Surround yourself with people of higher standards:*** If the people you closely relate with

have lower standards than yours, it is most likely that you will drop your standards so as to come to their level. In the same vein, when the people that are close to you have higher standards, you will be forced to up your game because these ones do not accept mediocrity of any sort. These ones would hold you to a higher standard than you hold yourself. You see why your relationships are very vital to your growth and development. We will dwell more on the role of the relationships that you have in coming chapters.

In this chapter, I would be sharing some of my basic standards that has directed the course of my life so far. These are my personal walls.

Bear in mind that we all have to create our individual unique standards. Remember that what works for one might not be applicable to another, as our stories and journeys are different. However, there are underlying fundamental principles to note.

Know Your Environment

To the most possible extent, I make efforts to be abreast with the happenings around me. I make conscious efforts to ensure that I am not in aloofness to the events in my environment. This is something that has stuck with me over the years. I can't be in isolation of the occurrences in any environment I find myself. I may not know the latest everything, but I always have an idea of what is evolving, what's new? What policies or laws have changed in my immediate environment and by extension, in the world at large? A piece of advice from me to you, try to know something about everything. I don't mean being snoopy. In relevant issues of everyday life, as it has to do with the present-day government, industry, education, agriculture, technology, etc, be informed. Be vast in knowledge. Be interested. Never be cut off from the rest of the world.

Have A Winning Mindset

There's not one success story that hasn't got some set back moments. I am not afraid of missing it. I give it my best and if I miss it, I try again. That way, I have learnt a way it wouldn't work, so I will re-strategize. Most fear of falling often arises from the doubt of the ability to get back up. If you were able to do it before, you sure can do it again. This time, in a better way because you must have learnt from the setback. You don't necessarily have to experience a setback to learn. No, you don't. You can walk in wisdom and get it right on point the very first time. Of course, it is possible. I always tell myself that the story wouldn't be complete until I get it; until I win. I would rather live with the memories of my adventures than the regret of not even trying. See setbacks as tools to get it right. Never give up and never give in. Never let it weigh you down. Success has many layers, uncover it bit by bit.

Respect Other People's Opinion

Give up the need to always be right. When it's worth it, choose rather to win a relationship than to win an argument. In fact, quit arguing. You are not wrong and sometimes, they are not wrong too. It's just that the views differ and as such, opinions differ too. This was a hard nut for me to crack but I am grinding it so smooth now. Most times, it's not about who is right or who is wrong. People have different perspective which may have been influenced by their peculiar experiences.

Often listen to understand and not to judge. Be as flexible as you can, try to see things from the perspective of others. Believe me, you will learn so much from that. There are often two views on any matter: a higher understanding and a lesser one. Know where you are and respect where others are.

What You Say Is As Important As How You Say It

I have come to realize that people may forget what you say to them but then may never let go of how you made them feel. No matter what I want to communicate, I try to do that in such a way that it becomes inspiring to the listener, that they take positive actions almost immediately and most importantly, without hurting their self-esteem.

What you say is important, how you say it is also important. Never talk to anyone in a condescending manner irrespective of their shortcomings. No one should leave your presence feeling worse. They should leave knowing that they need to step up their game. They should leave feeling like though they didn't give their best, they have the opportunity to do it better next time.

The "how you say it" is the packaging of your content (what you want to say) and it should be in such a way that it is appealing and acceptable; in a way that the message is not lost or fall on stony soils. Thus, not producing what it should.

I Don't Like You; It Doesn't Matter

Who likes me or who doesn't like me doesn't validate me. I don't lose sleep over who doesn't like me. If you like me, I like you. If you don't like me, I like you still but from afar. Everybody isn't going to like you because you cannot please everybody. The moment you try to please everybody, you gradually begin to lose your own self. Being a people pleaser has not done any good to anyone. Just be good and always do what's right.

Some people are going to like you and some people wouldn't, for reasons best known to them. It doesn't matter. Be good to them still. Be yourself; you can't really be yourself if you are busy moulding yourself into someone else's idea of being likeable. Ever heard that human wants are insatiable- you can't even completely satisfy a single human being, talk less of a lot of people.

The truth is that you are extremely likeable to the people that click with your vibes; wanting to be liked by all is so unhealthy. The only person you really need to impress is the person you see when you look in the mirror. The more you let yourself be who you are rather than aim to please everybody, the more attractive you will become.

When No One Is Watching

This reminds me of a story of a sculptor who after moulding a particular image, noticed a slight fault in the nose of the image. Because of this fault, the sculptor dismantled the image and started all over again, just to ensure that every detail of the image is exact and accurate.

When he was asked why he put that much effort considering the fact that where the image would be mounted is over 6 feet above ground level where no one would spot the error. He replied and said, "if no one knows the fault is there, I know the fault is there". This has left me with one principle. How you do what you do, when no one is watching is actually who you really are.

It's not about who is watching, it's about the character of your personality; what you are building yourself to be, what you are becoming. Always do the right thing even when no one is watching. This will help you cultivate an excellent attitude to learning, to work and to life. Trust me, it will make you exceptional.

Create Your Own Footprints

There are a thousand and one ways to kill a cat. It doesn't have to always be the usual way. Likewise, there are a thousand and one ways to accomplish any given feat. Find out other ways it can be done. Do you know how much I like to hear "this is the first time I am seeing this like this".

Be innovative- the conventional way you are used to is a product of someone's creative thinking. It's possible that it's been ages that happened. Always ask "What more can be done?" Get a better way, a richer way and a faster way. There is always a better way. Find it. Improve on existing methods or create new methods. Create your own footprints so that others will be better by it.

It's Impossible Until It Is Done

This is one of the Great Mandela's quotes. When a feat is considered impossible, chances are nobody ever accomplished such, but once someone does, it no longer becomes impossible. When I hear something is impossible to achieve, the first thing that comes to mind is "Oh! Nobody ever did this?" That makes it more interesting for me to dare. So, when you hear that something is impossible, never think that your ability is being undermined. Rather, conclude that whoever said that just expressed their fear and also informed you that you will be the first to do it once you get it accomplished. See it this way. Everything is possible once it is done.

The Whole Staircase

If you are to climb a four-storey building using the staircase, do you need to see the whole stairs one by one before you start climbing? The most possible answer is "No". You would discover that as you begin to climb, the rest of the stairs becomes more visible. The journey becomes clearer and looks easier too.

The same applies when you have a task, the moment you begin, a lot will be made clearer and then you keep moving until you achieve that which you want to. The rule here is to move, don't try to get it all figured out. When you take the first step, it will guide you on how to go about the second step.

Once you have a reasonable amount of information required for your journey, start moving immediately. I want to be a singer, start singing now and harness your skills on the go. You want to be anything? Start! You want to do anything? Start! Planning is a must, but do not wait to have all the facts and resources before you begin. Start with what you have, start with what you can and watch your journey become clearer and easy to relate with and if necessary, make adjustments on the go. A lot will unfold as you make progress.

There Is A Lesson In Everything

I learn from everything, from everyone and in anywhere. In waiting, I learn patience with a calm disposition. I hope you know that's a virtue. Look out for valuable lessons from your experiences with people and situations. Good experiences are made.

Bad experiences are also made. In all, I have something to learn. I love to play candy crush during my spare time; it's one of the ways I relax. One thing I have learnt from this game is that you don't know what's in the next level until you conquer and win your current level. So, is there a higher level? Yes. How does one get there? The answer is simple. Win your current level.

You see, even in playing a game, I have learnt a striking life lesson. There is a lesson in everything. Have this mentality and you will never lose because you will either win or you will learn.

Be A Good Forgiver

Yes! Be a good forgiver. Yes! I said that and it was no way in error. Do not be an expert in grudge and malice keeping. Do not seek revenge. When you get offended by people, try to maintain calmness. It might not be about you. They may be going through a lot at the time being and it just happened that you were the closest vent they had. Understand this and you will be happier. Make excuses for people.

That doesn't make you weak and doesn't suggest that you should often expose yourself to such engagements. What you do with such people is to keep them at a distance, especially if it continues and they are not repentant. Over the years, I have learnt to receive apologies that were never given; not because I was dumb but because I deserve my peace.

Holding unto an offence is too much load to carry and you need to journey as light as you can for the victories that are ahead of you. Don't keep records of wrongdoing. Let it go. Be a good "forgetter". Success demands it.

Never Again

It is possible that there are times that I might err; in dealing with people, in carrying out a task or in the process of executing a project. The "error" however, whatever it is, does not define me and will not cloud the way I see myself. I don't try to erase or cancel the error. I just do the right thing thereafter. I just do the opposite of the "erring". These are two different actions.

Let me explain, what is done is already done and can't be erased from records. Somehow, history will have it that the error occurred, especially if it included another person. So, I just tell myself. Never again! This won't happen again. And then I go ahead to do all that is necessary to appease the persons that have been affected by the action, with all remorsefulness and sincerity of heart.

An error does not define me. Trying to cover up an error, so it doesn't become obvious to the people around at the time, can get you to take irrational actions. Instead of covering up, correct the action. Just do the right thing. It doesn't matter how you are lashed at because of the "erring", do not let it get to you. Simply tell yourself that this won't ever repeat itself. If the mistake occurs and you are by yourself, fine and good, learn from it, move on to the next and only share to the world when if it would inspire someone in similar situation. Otherwise, keep it to yourself, this is your private victory.

Who remembers when we started to write with ink in primary school, and then there's a mistake, we try to cancel and cancel and cancel, eventually ending up with a more messed up paper. That's what happens when we try to cancel any error. What are you supposed to do then? Just cross the mistake, move on to the next and do the correct thing. In trying to cancel errors, we mess more things up.

These are just a few of the standards that I live by; some have had for years while some just surfaced recently as improvements on my person and some more will come in my journey of becoming. They should be inexhaustible.

Nonetheless, standards are necessary, and it is so important that you have them and live by them. Some of them, you don't have to announce as it will be clearly seen in the way you carry yourself and in your dealings. Choosing to raise your standards are entirely up to you. Remember that you won't sink below your standards and you won't rise above them too. You don't get what you want in life, you get what you accept. Have high standards, live by them and your life will rise to meet them.

CHAPTER 6

YOUR CIRCLE

"If you want to kill giants, follow a giant killer"

Bill Johnson

Relationships are vital part of human existence. No man has ever been reported to have come into this world by falling from the sky and landing on planet Earth. This is very unrealistic except in fictional movies. I said this to say that every human was born into an already existing family. We all have family members that we relate with, they are our first associates.

Your circle is about the people you relate with; the people that are involved in your life. This is your relationship circle.

Who Is In Your Circle?

A relationship circle helps us to determine who we know, how we know them, how often we see them or keep in touch with them, to what degree are they involved in our lives and how these people in our circle can spur us to being the best version of ourselves, reach the peak of our potentials and live the life that we desire through opportunities and support in whatever format that they may present.

Generally, people are related to one another either by blood (as family members) or by association (as friends, colleagues, neighbours, acquaintances). In this book, we will classify relationships into three zones:

- Family
- Friends
- Acquaintances

With you at the centre of these zones, the people in your life will often fall into any of the zones mentioned above.

For our first associates, our family, we don't get to choose the family we are born into. So, we just get to grow amongst a certain group of people who we have come to accept as father, mother, brothers and sisters as the case may be- they make up our immediate biological family. These are relationships acquired by birth. During our formative years, our immediate families are mostly involved in our lives. They are closest to us. They can tell how we took our first step when we started walking, the day our first set of teeth showed up, the first words we ever spoke; they know us from cradle. As we grow into childhood, we begin to play with other kids in our neighbourhood and in the schools we attend. When our parents visit their friends and they take us along, we get to play with the kids there also.

Eventually, even as kids we begin to get picky; we begin to have kids and cliché we prefer to be with. We now begin to have our favourite friends. Maybe because they make us feel a special kind of special, love us more than others (we think), they spend more time with us and they play the kind of play that we enjoy. Funny right? But how true! Even in our various schools, in our classes, we have our "friends" and others are "classmates". These classmates fall into the zone of acquaintances; they are people we get to see on a day to day basis and maybe spend some time with.

In life, they are ever present as colleagues, team members, course mates and the list can go on and on. They are in our outer circle; they may not really know you well and their names may just be the only thing you know about them, but then, work has brought you together; an assigned project has unified your purposes for the time being. Depending on how often you relate, the more you get to know them better, chances are that they may move to the friends' zone.

Choosing Your Friends

A lot of times, what is important to a person will usually determine who is important to them. People are often drawn to minds of common interest- people who they share common values and beliefs with. What is important to a person most probably would be revealed in their vision; you see why having a clear defined vision and purpose for your life is important. It doesn't just guide the direction you go in life but also will help you choose your friends and the company you keep.

By the time you as a person is so clear about what you are about in life, you would naturally be drawn to people who are too, and who are disciplined in it. You would decline from hanging out with people who do not know what they want in life. Nothing would satisfy you in such associations.

Having friends and hanging out with friends shouldn't just be about play and fun, friends should add value to your life, and you should also be valuable to your friends. When choosing friends, try not to limit yourself to your peers; have friends that influence you positively and have friends that you can positively influence. Have them older than you, in another level that is not yours; have them younger than you in another class that is different from yours. That way, you would be able to share vast experiences with one another, one to prepare you for where you are yet to be or to prepare someone else in your crew.

Choosing your friends is not a onetime event but a practice which allows you to carefully study the people that come around you and then decide within you which of them will stay close as your friend and which you may have to keep at a distance. Not because they are terrible people but maybe because you are still unsure about them. You don't have to come to their faces and say "I choose you, I wouldn't choose you", that might erupt unnecessary and avoidable enmity.

When you have decided who you want as a friend, then spending quality time, creating healthy habits and finding hobbies you share together would help concretize the friendship. Friends come and go. Yes! But individuals who have mastered the ability to consciously decide who come into their lives, who stay, who leaves, who they stay in touch with, are mostly successful in building meaningful relationships. So, you see, it's still all up to you.

Your Front Row

This is simply about influence and vibes. Don't you think those relationships that give positive vibes should be in your front row? While those that frequently give negative vibes should be relegated to the background where they will gradually be starved until they no longer matter and exist.

Look at it critically, the people who are often front row worthy, earned it over time as they must have proven themselves to be of so much value and support; they are close enough to see all your flaws and setbacks as it may be, yet, they chose to feed your strengths and amplify your beauties. And over time, they have watched you evolve. Because these ones chose to see what diamond can be made out of this coal. They keep cheering you onto greater heights. They don't talk you down. They don't make you feel less. They spread so much hope, love and happiness. These ones are on our VIP list, they give us wings to fly as we reach beyond the skies. These ones are front row worthy. So, I ask you again. Who is in your front row?

"Life is a theatre. Invite your audience carefully. Not everyone is healthy enough to have a front row seat in our lives. There are some people in your life that need to be loved from a distance. It's amazing what you can accomplish when you let go, or at least minimize your time with draining, negative, incompatible, not- going-anywhere relationships and friendships. Observe the relationships around you. Pay attention. Which one lifts and which one leans? Which ones encourage and which ones discourage? Which ones are on a path of growth uphill and which ones are going downhill? When you leave certain people, do you feel better or do you feel worse? Which ones always have drama, or don't really understand, know or appreciate you? The more you seek quality, respect, growth, peace of mind, love and truth around you, the easier it will become for you to decide who gets to sit in the front row and who should be moved to the balcony of your life. You cannot change the people around you but you can change the people you are around" –Anonymous.

A Class Of Their Own

Talking about your relationship circle would be incomplete without highlighting the significance of having mentors and role models. Now, as you can see, they do not fall into any of the relationship zones aforementioned. They are in a class of their own. They are a must have in your relationship circle and many at times, they come with a price; might be something you pay in the place of service as you volunteer to work with them and learn by personal contact (in the case of a mentor) or something you get to pay with your devoted time by studying their lives, actions, results as you learn by observation and imitation (in the case of a role model). After all, everything has got a price. The question now is, is it worth it?

One thing I can guarantee you is, this one is more than worth it. Find out the price you may need to pay and pay it in full. It is one of the ways you invest in the inner you. It will pay off now and in the nearest future.

Let's differentiate between these two- Mentors and role models. A role model is a person you look up to, admire so much and have greatly been inspired by his or her works, acts, deeds, words and the way they have built their lives. They are reputable, accomplished and successful individuals who have lived an impactful life (that is if they are dead) or are still making giant strides in their chosen endeavour (that is if they are living). They can be someone you have never met in person. They can be from any part of this world. The most important thing is that you know their story and you would love to emulate their styles. So you get to read about them, watch videos and listen to audios about them, how they do what they do and what their drive was or still is as the case may be.

On the other hand, mentors are people you learn from by personal contact in whatever format. They must be living as at the period of mentoring. That means that you know them, and they know you. And they know that they are mentoring you. In this case, it is a two-way relationship which also demands for a two-way communicating pattern.

They are also reputable individuals who are doing outstandingly great in their chosen field of life. They are inspiring and you have considered them fit and worthy to mentor you because you want to achieve their kind of results or better still outlive them. Sometimes, they are in a similar or same field of life that you are aiming to venture into. Sometimes, they are individuals who have been trained, are skilful and have gathered a wealth of experience to help you through a phase of life that they have surmounted significantly.

Personally, one striking difference between a mentor and a role model is that since role models may not know you as a person and may be dead, you don't get them to answer some questions that you may have with respect to why they did certain things in certain ways, but for a mentor, you get to have all your questions answered gradually in your work and walk with them. Here, you get the advantage of both the training and the education.

Role models are a must have. Mentors are a must get. It cannot be overemphasized. Be grateful when you get a mentor especially and learn all that you can because you would not forever be mentored. Just like a football coach, they help you learn all the skills and tricks to win the game but then, you would have to play without them. Having role models and mentors in your circle would give you a broader perspective over a lot of issues of life.

You may not achieve much all by yourself or by working solo. That's why you need quality relationships, as they make room for you to learn and grow in your purpose. Have valuable friends, be a valuable friend, keep valuable companies. Build healthy and meaningful relationships.

CHAPTER 7

YOUR CARRIAGE

"Never bend your head. Always hold it high. Look the
world straight in the eye"

Hellen Keller

ow do you walk into a room? How do you sit?
How do you move? How do you stand? How
are you showing up? In standing, do you cover
up the space that you are in or do you shrink into a corner
or do you rest on something for support? In sitting, do you
often sit straight, or do you often sink into the chair?

In moving, do you move confidently or are you scared to
carry your steps or are you always nervous when you have
to move around people? In showing up, are you expressing
happiness or sadness, or are you active or passive? All of
these are nonverbal communications of yours that are
sending messages to your subconscious and to the people
around you.

Picture this scenario; you are in a hall with about fifty other persons for example, and then someone just walks in and you noticed that this person got a hold of the attention of everyone in the hall, including you. Not one person could stop to stare at this individual and some are even asking "who is this?" This person commands attention in a fascinating way, from the way he or she is dressed, to the way they walked in and the way they exude confidence. It's called Carriage.

Carriage describes the way in which a person keeps or moves their body when they are standing, sitting, walking or even talking. It is a combination of posture, gesture, confidence, charisma, mood and personal presence. This put together communicates your personality to others and gives an impression of you, even before you open your mouth to say a word.

So, let me ask you a question, what impression is the way you carry yourself giving? What is it communicating to others? Does it make others want to come around you? Does it show arrogance? Does it show self-doubt? Does it create a warm reception? You need to find out and adjust accordingly.

Most times, your carriage is an unconscious expression. This is because it is to a large extent a reflection of your mental disposition at a given point in time- how you see yourself, how you see others and how you see the world altogether. This is where yourself value and how you value others gives expression unconsciously. Your carriage can be seen in your body languages, speech mannerisms, appearance, conduct, mood, conversations and behaviours. We would be looking at these vices of carriage and also guide you into being more conscious of how they say so much about you.

Body Languages

These are nonverbal elements in our communication that we use to reveal our innermost feelings, emotions, opinions or our state of mind. Through body languages, we send signals and speak to others with our bodily movements like posture, eye contact, hand gestures and facial expressions. They communicate without us saying a word. Body languages can alter or emphasize the meaning of the spoken language we use in communicating. So, without knowing it, we may be communicating what we don't mean to. Hence, it becomes important that we master our body languages and use them when need be to express our exact intentions, feelings and opinions.

Body languages are mainly used when we are communicating face to face not when you are on a phone call except it is a video call when you get to see the person on the other line on your device screen.

Depending on what our body languages communicate, they can have a positive or negative impact on the people around us as well as ourselves. For example, maintaining eye contact with the person you are talking with helps you appear confident, make them feel comfortable and interested in what you are saying. Looking at the floor on the other hand, can make you appear weak and unsure of that which you are talking about. Unless, what you are talking about is on the floor. That's one.

Another one. As a teenager, I learnt about walking briskly; not too fast and not too slow but walking as if you are headed to an important destination. Because you are actually heading somewhere. Never walk sluggishly. Chin up! Chest out! Straight your shoulders! And walk with poise always, irrespective of who is watching. Remember, it's not about who is watching since we are not in a show.

It's about presenting yourself as that charismatic personality that you are.

From the way you are staring, to the way you scratch your head when you are asked a question, to the way you snuggle your nose, to the way you squint your eyes, to the way you bite your lower lip, to the way you put your hand under your chin, to the way you fold your hands on your chest, to the way tilt your head to one side, to your partial smile, to the way you cross your legs while sitting and to the tone and pace of your speeches. All of these are already communicating.

This is just a few of the numerous body languages that do exist. You may need to learn more about body languages from personal research. This will be the first step in helping you send the right body language messages. However, since you want to have productive interactions with the people you relate with, it is important that you strive towards understanding your own self and the people around you as it will be detrimental to depend solely on body languages.

Develop your qualities as a person so that naturally the people in your life would get to see what a smart, intelligent, warm, social and wonderful fellow you really are.

Speech Mannerisms

This refers to the way we express ourselves in words. It goes beyond what is said but also considers how it is said. How we say what we say is a product of our speech mannerisms. In whatever language that we know to speak, each and every one of us have a manner of speaking. We differ from our choice of words, the pronunciation of words, tone of speech and pace of speech.

Some people speak very fast while some people speak very slow; others are extremely loud while for others, we may need to pull a little bit closer just to grasp their words. All of these are speech habits, obviously not appropriate. Thus, they can be adjusted so as to ensure we communicate right to our listeners. Balance is unavoidable when it comes to our speech manners.

Also, our choice of words is important. Avoid offensive words; offensive words are not necessarily abusive words. There are certain words considered as vulgar, find out about them and totally eliminate them from your vocabulary. Learn also to pronounce words correctly. Discover appealing speech manners and utilize them. Always speak with confidence and let not idle words proceed out of your mouth. Mean what you say and say only what you mean. When you are pulling a prank or making a joke, please clarify afterwards. What you say is who you are. Here are a few appealing speech habits to cultivate:

•	Be courteous always

•	Show politeness

•	Learn to use "please, thank you and you are welcome"

•	Use respectful words

•	Speak and let others speak also

Conduct

Every human, irrespective of their ages is to an extent is aware of what's wrong, what's right, what's morally acceptable and what's not. This in our subconscious, tend to guide the way we conduct ourselves with family, friends, relatives, neighbours, colleagues and the society at large.

Often times, a person's conduct is a build-up of how they have interacted at individual events, circumstances and situations- a reflection of how they have behaved over time. This then forms their character. One's character is a total evaluation of their stable moral qualities that have played out over time.

However, you look at it, character is a combination of those qualities that distinguishes an individual from another. They are personal habits. When an individual is said to have a good character, it points to the existence of more good virtues or good habits or good behaviour. Reversely, when an individual is said to have a bad character, it points to the lack of more good virtues, good habits or good behaviour.

Every human being has the ability to portray good character or bad character. The choice is always there, whether you chose intentionally or not. This brings to mind a caption I saw on a magazine some years ago, it read: "In each of us is the good wolf and the bad wolf. The wolf you feed consistently is the one that grows and form the basis of your character". How true!

Cultivate good habits, nurture them and grow in them. Evaluate yourself every now and then, do away with any trait of the bad wolf. Inculcate virtues like honesty, modesty, empathy, gratitude, loyalty, patience, meekness and humility. They will make you relate better with people and you will become an incredible person to be with.

Appearance

How do you look? How do you dress? How do you groom? What's your mood? Simply put, appearance is the way you look which is a put together of how you dress, how you groom and the mood that you carry; especially when you appear in public. Dressing defines the way you wear your clothes – your dress sense. Grooming describes all the things you do to make your appearance look clean and tidy. It is a detailed care for one's appearance, personal hygiene and clothing.

The major thing here is how you take care of yourself – your body, from the strand of the hair on your head to the soles of your feet. Grooming shouldn't be expensive; you don't necessarily have to own the most expensive of clothing and toiletries to be a well-groomed person. It is more of how you keep clean and neat with that which you already have and can afford comfortably.

In life, it is even the way we handle seemingly small things smarter that have a significant impact on the quality of life we live. From how you wear what you wear, to your choice of grooming products and tools you consider quality that can give you the desired outcome.

Have a grooming routine that you can't skip. I can't imagine someone taking a bath without a body wash (soap or shower gel). There are certain everyday personal hygiene practices that shouldn't be skipped. You can't afford to be a public nuisance as a result of forgetting to brush your teeth. This is not funny? Really, you can't afford it. How can you forget? These things should be a part of you. Take care of your body. Smell nice always. Feel good in your own skin.

Talking about your mood, this is a crucial factor that contributes to your appearance in the most undeniable way. Imagine someone all dressed up, looking nice and smelling nice too. Then, comes into a meeting looking so sad and unhappy. Now, the focus is definitely going to shift from how nice he or she looks to the mood they appeared with. The people around them will be trying to find out what went wrong with them before they came into the meeting. Really? What went wrong? Yes, because their mood has expressed that something is wrong.

As much as you can, do not carry a negative mood around. It is possible that something unexpected has occurred and then it makes you unhappy. Try not to show up with such sadness especially with people who are not related to the matter at hand or with people who don't have any role to play to remedy or avert such unappealing situation. Moods are contagious. You can just show up crying and everybody else around you are now trying all they can not to join you in crying. You can show up with all smiles are the people that are frowning before you came in just switch to smiles too.

Ever wondered why the hostesses on an airplane are always warm, friendly and looking happy. It is because they have been trained to ensure that anyone that comes in contact with them on the airplane is made most comfortable with the presence of joy and warmth that they are expected to always carry. These hostesses are obligated and compelled to always show up smiling, no matter what is going wrong with them or around them.

Do you think that they don't have personal challenges that they may even be facing at that point in time? Whatever it is, they always carry a warm and appealing atmosphere.

You can take a cue from that. Carrying a sad face has never solved any problem.

Seek out for productive ways to solve or tackle any challenge; maybe by talking to someone who you consider worthy and will have a solution to what the issue is. It is important that you always show up in your most appealing mood. You are the best of you; always show up as your best self.

Conclusion

YOU GOT THIS!

At this point, I want to personally congratulate you for making it to this page; for taking the time to read all seven chapters of this book. Every page must have left you thinking, learning and reminding you of other things not mentioned in this book, but then has got to do with your life and you may need to give them more attention.

I believed this journey has been worthwhile and you have gained so much knowledge. Now, it's time to put to practice all that you have learnt; it's time to take all you have learnt and start functioning with them. It's time to put into action all you have concluded in your mind, those resolutions you came up with and those new goals you set.

You must have heard that "knowledge is power" but have you also heard that "applied knowledge is power". I totally agree with the latter; of course, the former is also correct, but it is a lesser truth. The latter is the greater truth. Power to cause dynamic changes often lies with the application of new information.

Why do you think a lot of people might be exposed to same knowledge by same teacher and yet, just a handful of them is able to make something out of it. It is because of the immediate application of knowledge acquired. Underline the word "immediate". Yes! It has to be immediately. No procrastination of any sort. This is what will distinguish you from others. Strike the iron now while it is still hot. What you do with what you know is all that counts. I tell you, you got this!

Now that you know that the quality of life you will live is largely dependent on the quality of your inner man- the quality of your mind. Always concentrate more on this inner you, always invest in it by exposing it to the right and necessary contents that will enrich and prepare you for this beautiful life you will live. All your dreams and aspirations are valid and achievable. Who you become in the place of learning will mould you into a person of value. What do you offer to the world? Your value will attract men of honour, men of power, men of wisdom and men of fortunes.

Honestly, the good things of life were never meant to be pursued, they are to be attracted. So, work more on being a person of value because when you are a person of immeasurable value, you will have more than enough to afford the kind of life that you want to have. The life of so much plenty and abundance.

However, there's so much to life than just accumulating so much for you and all of yours. As much as these needs are important that you meet them for you and for the people that are related to you, it is important that you also reach out to contribute in the most possible way that you can to the basic needs of the people in your world. Apart from this, you will only be surviving and not living a significant life.

A significant life is the life that affect others positively; not just the people that are related to you but others too, that may not be able to even afford the basic needs of life. That's living a life of impact. The more wealth and fortune you accumulate, the more impact you should make in your world. That is honouring your call; your call to making this world a better place. You will surely live in plenty, wealth and abundance, but also give back to humanity and lift others too. Live an inspiring life. Live a modest life. And I tell you, you got this!

One final thing, it is the extra factor that gives you a beyond the natural advantage; the extra ordinary factor that comes into play in your plans, dreams, goals and purpose, and becomes the deal maker. Some call it good luck, some call it fate, some call it coincidence. I call it God's Grace. As far as God is concerned, your future is history. He has seen it all from the beginning, he knows exactly what you should do. That's why you should invite Him into the affairs of your life, so He will guide you all through the way.

First, you must acknowledge that there's more to this world that meets the eyes. Isn't it fantastic that when you need like five steps to get something done, then on your second step, something happens that defiles the usual process and still gets the job done in lesser time than you have imagined. You can't exactly explain this, you know it is not your doing. It just happened in your favour. Someone would say it's magic. To me, that's God's Grace at work. When you take the first step, God's Grace steps in.

This is the supernatural power that crowns all your efforts with outstanding results. I know this is real because this is the life that I live, and I am grateful every day for the gift of Jesus. He has made my life so beautiful and He can make yours too. He will hold you by the hand and take you places. With Jesus, there is no fear of tomorrow. With Jesus, there is no uncertainty of the future.

So, are you ready to make Jesus the pilot of your life?

I can hear a resounding YES!

Just say these words out, mean each one from your heart. Say:

Dear Lord God, I believe in Jesus, that He is the son of God and that He is alive today. I proclaim that from this day, Jesus is Lord of my life. I trust Him with my life. I am confident that with Jesus, I would be a wonder to my world. Thank you Father for I know that you have heard me.

And that's it, Congratulations!

Now, you have a tag team, a super force team. He is now in your relationship circle, in fact, He is in your front row.

There's so much exploit you will wrath.

Ahead! Ahead! You go. See you at the top.

GoGirl! You have all it takes.

ABOUT THE AUTHOR

Loveth Omotola is an award-winning social entrepreneur, Educationist, Author, Personal Development Coach and a Success motivational speaker. Through her expose` as a core value specialist, she educates young people in Nigeria on the importance of having the right set of values and its influence on their goals setting, decision making and practical living. In volunteering with Voluntary Service Overseas (VSO Nigeria), and seeing the gap in the awareness of global social needs.

She begun a movement in Nigeria to enlighten teenagers and young adults on being more conscious of their environment and the roles each one of them can play in making the world a better place through their contributions towards the achievement of the Sustainable Development Goals.

She is also the Founder of GLOW INITIATIVE FOR GIRLS' EDUCATION; a Non-profit organization that champions girls education in Nigeria and by extension, Africa. GLOW INITIATIVE FOR GIRLS' EDUCATION advocates that Education be prioritized; as it targets girls who are least likely to receive education due to poverty, geographical location, traditions and long held beliefs that do not support formal education for girls. Through this initiative, she has successfully executed several community development projects as it relates to the overall well-being of the girl child and has inspired over 5000 girls in the past 5 years, towards learning and acquisition of skills and knowledge that give rise to personal development. She is very passionate about seeing girls and women take up spaces of leadership in various industry of life.

During leisure, she is an adventurous person; loves to climb mountains, enjoys traveling, bike touring, canoeing, healthy cooking, seeing movies and listening to good music.

CONNECT WITH ME

Thank you for buying and reading this book. Please remember to leave reviews and connect with me on my social media platforms.

Mail: speak2omotolaloveth@gmail.com

Instagram: @lovethomotolahallmarks

Facebook: Loveth Omotola

INVEST IN GIRLS WITH US

Having purchased this book, you are helping us put funds together to send a girl somewhere in Africa to school. Hence, your financial support is a means to an end. Be a part of this lofty project to actualize a dependable legacy for a girl's future through your partnership. Join us to send girls to school! Donate to this cause.

Through education, we give her a pen to rewrite her story and a voice to share it with the world and inspire others.

Connect with us on our social media platforms.

Mail: glowgirlinitiative@gmail.com

Instagram: @glowgirlinitiative

Facebook: GlowGirl Initiative